C0-EEQ-051

GLIMPSES OF GOD'S PRESENCE

Glimpses of God's Presence

CAROLYN RHEA

BROADMAN PRESS

Nashville, Tennessee

© Copyright 1978 • Broadman Press.

All rights reserved.

4251-63

ISBN: 0-8054-5163-3

Dewey Decimal Classification: 811

Subject Headings: RELIGIOUS POETRY // MEDITATIONS

Library of Congress Catalog Card Number: 77-26533

Printed in the United States of America

To
these loved ones

Boyd and Mary Turnage

Claude and Cecile Rhea

Mudge Dye

About the Author

Carolyn Rhea is a free-lance writer and author from Birmingham, Alabama. She has published a number of inspirational books, including her previous Broadman book, *Healing in His Wings*.

She is also a public-school teacher. She is married to Claude H. Rhea, dean of the School of Music, Samford University. They have three children, Randy, Meg, and Claude (called C^3).

Mrs. Rhea is best known for her poems which relate the Bible to everyday living.

Contents

Prologue 11

IN THE BEGINNING
    Holy Ground 14
    Shadows of the Almighty 16

ENCOUNTER WITH CHRIST
    Resurrection 20
    Metamorphosis 22
    The Way 24
    Middle C 26
    Complement 28
    Swath to Calvary 30
    Perspective 32

A GLIMPSE OF MY HEAVENLY FATHER
    Lineage 36
    Impressionistic Painting 38
    Full Shadow 40
    Trust 42

A GLIMPSE OF MYSELF
    Grafted 46
    Ebb Tide 48
    Scrabble 50
    Bright Lights of Happiness 52
    Conscience 54
    Christian Character 56
    Oil of Laughter 58
    Conservation 60
    Eclipse 62
    Blueprint 64
    Key of C 66
    Apogees of Joy 68

A GLIMPSE OF OTHERS
  Vulnerable 72
  Lovely Rooms 74
  Within the Lines 76
  Flying Buttresses 78
  Weapons 80
  Hygrometer 82
  Environment 84
  Freedom 86
  Growing in Thy Will 88
  Fulcrum 90
  In Jesus' Name 92
  Propelled 94
  Shoes of Discipleship 96

A GLIMPSE OF THE HOLY SPIRIT
  Kinetic Energy 100
  Spiritual Hearing Aid 102
  Tightrope of Temptation 104
  Interpreter 106

A GLIMPSE OF THE CHURCH
  Orchard 110
  Money Changers 112
  Citizens of the Kingdom 114
  Reflecting 116
  Tributaries 118

REVELATION
  Spectrum 122
  Thy Shadow 124
  When Life Is Felled 126

Epilogue 128

GLIMPSES OF GOD'S PRESENCE

Prologue

> God, where are you?
> Ignite my burning bush
> And make your presence known!

But there is total darkness ("No man hath seen God at any time"—John 1:18) *until I encounter Jesus Christ* ("the only begotten Son, which is in the bosom of the Father, he hath declared him"—John 1:18).

In the light of Christ's presence, I am able to glimpse "shadows of the Almighty" here on earth and to abide therein. There could be no shadows, though, without his light. "I am come a light into the world, that whosoever believeth on me should not abide in darkness" (John 12:46).

Continuing my journey onward with Christ, I'll sail beyond earth's visible horizon into the glorious light of God's eternal presence.

> Who is the blessed and only Potentate, the King of kings, and Lord of lords; Who only hath immortality, dwelling in the light which no man can approach unto; whom no man hath seen, nor can see: to whom be honour and power everlasting. Amen (1 Tim. 6:15–16).

In the Beginning

And ye shall seek me, and find me, when ye shall search for me with all your heart (Jer. 29:13).

Holy Ground

God, where are you?
Ignite my burning bush
And make thy presence known!

Can it be there is no "holy ground"
   where thou canst visit me?

Help me clear away
   the underbrush of sin and selfishness
     and cultivate a heavenly plot
       within my soul
Where I can shed
   my shoes of sophistication
And humbly kneel,
   childlike again,
With mind still open to awe
And ears eager to listen.

Speak *then*, Lord, for thy servant heareth.

Glimpses . . .

And he said, Draw not nigh hither: put off thy shoes from off thy feet, for the place whereon thou standest is holy ground (Ex. 3:5).

Who shall ascend into the hill of the Lord? or who shall stand in his holy place? He that hath clean hands, and a pure heart; who hath not lifted up his soul unto vanity, nor sworn deceitfully (Ps. 24:3–4).

Draw nigh to God, and he will draw nigh to you. Cleanse your hands, ye sinners; and purify your hearts, ye double minded (Jas. 4:8).

The Lord is nigh unto all them that call upon him, to all that call upon him in truth (Ps. 145:18).

Let us therefore come boldly unto the throne of grace, that we may obtain mercy, and find grace to help in time of need (Heb. 4:16).

And ye shall seek me, and find me, when ye shall search for me with all your heart (Jer. 29:13).

Shadows of the Almighty

Almighty God, thy greatness
   is beyond the grasp of my frail mind;
Yet deep within there is this yearning
   to seek and find thee for myself.

I stumble in Earth's darkness.
My soul cries out for light.

These human eyes are not conditioned
   for the blinding light
     of thy glorious presence,
But perhaps they could discern
   thy *shadow* touching Earth.

Break through with *light*, O God!
I cannot see even a shadow
Unless there is some light!

Glimpses . . .

O send out thy light and thy truth: let them lead me (Ps. 43:3).

The entrance of thy words giveth light (Ps. 119:130).

In thy light shall we see light (Ps. 36:9).

Open thou mine eyes, that I may behold wondrous things out of thy law (Ps. 119:18).

That they should seek the Lord, if haply they might feel after him, and find him, though he be not far from every one of us (Acts 17:27).

When thou saidst, Seek ye my face; my heart said unto thee, Thy face, Lord, will I seek (Ps. 27:8).

Seek, and ye shall find: knock, and it shall be opened unto you (Matt. 7:7).

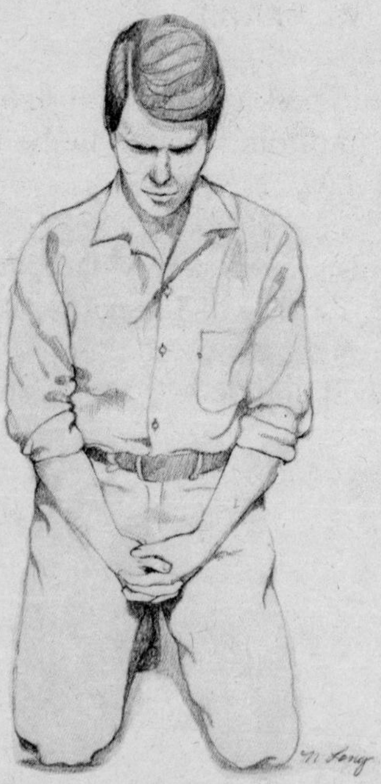

Encounter with Christ

He that seeth me seeth him that sent me. I am come a light into the world, that whosoever believeth on me should not abide in darkness (John 12:45–46).

While ye have light, believe in the light, that ye may be the children of light (John 12:36).

Resurrection

I stand in the umbra [1] of the cross
   and see myself as I truly am:
      Weak, wavering,
      Encrusted with scales of sin,
      Slave to the evil one who rules my flesh
         and holds my spirit captive,
      Heir only to death.

But with Easter's dawning light
I see an empty tomb!
My spirit leaps with joy!
Not *death*—but *resurrection*!

Humbly I kneel in loving response.
The serpent in me sheds its skin
   and slithers away.
Reaching out to Christ, whose love
   has freed my spirit and
      resurrected my life,
I rise to walk with dignity and worth
   in his kingdom here on earth.

---

[1] full shadow, total darkness

Glimpses . . .

I am come a light into the world, that whosoever believeth on me should not abide in darkness (John 12:46).

And as Moses lifted up the serpent in the wilderness, even so must the Son of man be lifted up: That whosoever believeth in him should not perish, but have eternal life (John 3:14–15).

And you hath he quickened, who were dead in trespasses and sins; Wherein in time past ye walked according to the course of this world, according to the prince of the power of the air, the spirit that now worketh in the children of disobedience: Among whom also we all had our conversation in times past in the lusts of our flesh, fulfilling the desires of the flesh and of the mind; and were by nature the children of wrath, even as others. But God, who is rich in mercy, for his great love wherewith he loved us, Even when we were dead in sins, hath quickened us together with Christ (by grace ye are saved); And hath raised us up together, and made us sit together in heavenly places in Christ Jesus (Eph. 2:1–6).

I am crucified with Christ: nevertheless I live; yet not I, but Christ liveth in me: and the life which I now live in the flesh I live by the faith of the Son of God, who loved me, and gave himself for me (Gal. 2:20).

Metamorphosis

Like a crawling caterpillar
   I make my entry upon earth.

Slowly I bind about myself
   the threads of sin and selfishness
Until I am encased in darkness.

God's love, though, reaches out
   and touches me through Christ
And frees me from my encircling cocoon.

I emerge a new creature
With wings to fly!

Glimpses . . .

Bring my soul out of prison, that I may praise thy name (Ps. 142:7).

Therefore if any man be in Christ, he is a new creature: old things are passed away; behold, all things are become new (2 Cor. 5:17).

I am come a light into the world, that whosoever believeth on me should not abide in darkness (John 12:46).

I am come that they might have life, and that they might have it more abundantly (John 10:10).

Unto you that fear my name shall the Sun of righteousness arise with healing in his wings; and ye shall go forth, and grow up (Mal. 4:2).

For the law of the Spirit of life in Christ Jesus hath made me free from the law of sin and death (Rom. 8:2).

The Way

I scan Earth's horizon,
As did Columbus long ago,
And hear the fearful cries
That life is flat
And Death's screaming drop-off
   ends it all!

But Christ reassures my faith
   that there is more.
Returning from his voyage beyond
   life's visible horizon,
He became the Way.

Aboard his seaworthy ship,
I'll sail earth's seas
   with zest and joy;
And, confident that life's horizon
   stretches on and on,
I'll journey with him
   through Death's disturbing darkness
And discover for myself
   the other side of eternity!

Glimpses . . .

Jesus saith unto him, I am the way, the truth, and the life: no man cometh unto the Father, but by me (John 14:6).

I came forth from the Father, and am come into the world: again, I leave the world, and go to the Father (John 16:28).

Yet a little while, and the world seeth me no more; but ye see me: because I live, ye shall live also (John 14:19).

Ye seek Jesus of Nazareth, which was crucified: he is risen; he is not here: behold the place where they laid him (Mark 16:6).

After that he appeared in another form unto two of them, as they walked, and went into the country (Mark 16:12).

So then after the Lord had spoken unto them, he was received up into heaven, and sat on the right hand of God (Mark 16:19).

Middle C

The keyboard of life lies before me.
Where and how do I begin?

With *Christ*, who is Middle C!
Oriented in him, I can learn
   to read the music God has written
And experience harmony within his will.

Thus there is meaning even in dissonant
      passages,
Haunting beauty in life's lovely melodies,
Joy in its magnificent crescendos,
Comfort in its rests,
And confidence in the growing skill
   of Christian maturity
      through Jesus Christ!

Glimpses . . .

That Christ may dwell in your hearts by faith; that ye, being rooted and grounded in love, May be able to comprehend with all saints what is the breadth, and length, and depth, and height; And to know the love of Christ, which passeth knowledge, that ye might be filled with all the fulness of God (Eph. 3:17–19).

For I have given you an example, that ye should do as I have done to you (John 13:15).

I am the vine, ye are the branches: He that abideth in me, and I in him, the same bringeth forth much fruit: for without me ye can do nothing (John 15:5).

That we henceforth be no more children, tossed to and fro, and carried about with every wind of doctrine, by the sleight of men, and cunning craftiness, whereby they lie in wait to deceive; But speaking the truth in love, may grow up into him in all things, which is the head, even Christ (Eph. 4:14–15).

Complement

Christ is the complement [2]
   my life needs for fulfillment.

Without him, I am oblique: [3]
   bent by sin and inadequacy.

But joined with him through faith,
I am brought into an upright relationship
   with God,
     with myself,
       and with my fellowman.

[2] something that completes or makes perfect; in mathematics, the amount needed to make an angle equal to 90 degrees (a right angle)
[3] more or less than 90 degrees

Glimpses . . .

I am the true vine, and my Father is the husbandman. Abide in me, and I in you. As the branch cannot bear fruit of itself, except it abide in the vine; no more can ye, except ye abide in me. I am the vine, ye are the branches: He that abideth in me, and I in him, the same bringeth forth much fruit: for without me ye can do nothing (John 15:1,4–5).

I am come that they might have life, and that they might have it more abundantly (John 10:10).

Take my yoke upon you, and learn of me; for I am meek and lowly in heart: and ye shall find rest unto your souls (Matt. 11:29).

Who is he that overcometh the world, but he that believeth that Jesus is the Son of God? (1 John 5:5).

I can do all things through Christ which strengtheneth me (Phil. 4:13).

Swath to Calvary

Thy love, O God,
   cut a swath to Calvary
     and to the empty tomb
And opened up the Way to thee.

Ascending that path
   of faith in Christ,
     who is the Way,
We reach the heights of a personal
     relationship with thee.

No longer mere creatures of thy hand,
We become thy sons and daughters!

Secure in the marvel of our new identity,
We walk with confidence
As thy family here on earth.

Glimpses . . .

God . . . hath in these last days spoken unto us by his Son, whom he hath appointed heir of all things, by whom also he made the worlds (Heb. 1:1–2).

Jesus saith unto him, I am the way, the truth, and the life: no man cometh unto the Father, but by me (John 14:6).

Having therefore, brethren, boldness to enter into the holiest by the blood of Jesus, By a new and living way, which he hath consecrated for us, through the veil, that is to say, his flesh; And having an high priest over the house of God; Let us draw near with a true heart in full assurance of faith (Heb. 10:19–22).

Enter ye at the strait gate . . . Because strait is the gate, and narrow is the way, which leadeth unto life, and few there be that find it (Matt. 7:13–14).

The Spirit itself beareth witness with our spirit, that we are the children of God: And if children, then heirs; heirs of God, and joint-heirs with Christ (Rom. 8:16–17).

Perspective

All I comprehend of thee
  at this moment, God,
  is limited to the *acute angle* [4]
  of my present existence.

Stretch these boundaries
  of mind
    and heart
      and soul
To encompass a larger view—
An ever-expanding *obtuse* perspective
Within life's *straight angle;*

For I am cognizant that life is
  but half the circle,
And only the *full circle* of eternity
  can reveal thee fully.

---

[4] An acute angle is less than 90 degrees; an obtuse angle, more than 90 degrees but less than 180 degrees. A straight angle has 180 degrees; a circle, 360 degrees.

Glimpses . . .

For now we see through a glass, darkly; but then face to face: now I know in part; but then shall I know even as also I am known (1 Cor. 13:12).

For thou art my lamp, O Lord: and the Lord will lighten my darkness (2 Sam. 22:29).

And I will bring the blind by a way that they knew not: I will lead them in paths that they have not known: I will make darkness light before them, and crooked things straight. These things will I do unto them, and not forsake them (Isa. 42:16).

Teach me thy way, O Lord, and lead me in a plain path (Ps. 27:11).

I will instruct thee and teach thee in the way which thou shalt go: I will guide thee with mine eye (Ps. 32:8).

Touching the Almighty, we cannot find him out (Job 37:23).

Great is our Lord, and of great power: his understanding is infinite (Ps. 147:5).

A Glimpse of My Heavenly Father

Philip saith unto him, Lord, shew us the Father . . . . Jesus saith unto him . . . he that hath seen me hath seen the Father . . . . Believe me that I am in the Father, and the Father in me (John 14:8–9,11).

Lineage

Child of earth and heaven am I.

Born of Mother Earth,
I am nourished in her bosom,
   childishly content.
Yet pulsing within me
   is the spiritual imprint
   of my heavenly Father's image
And a growing awareness of his
   presence and sustaining care.

So I am not content to sit forever
   in Mother Earth's
     comfortable lap
But shall stand and learn to walk
   on growing legs of faith;
And when he beckons from beyond,
I shall rush into my Heavenly Father's
   outstretched arms!

Glimpses . . .

Have we not all one father? hath not one God created us? (Mal. 2:10).

Ye are the sons of the living God (Hos. 1:10).

For in him we live, and move, and have our being; as certain also of your own poets have said, For we are also his offspring (Acts 17:28).

So God created man in his own image, in the image of God created he him; male and female created he them (Gen. 1:27).

That ye may be the children of your Father which is in heaven (Matt. 5:45).

Behold, what manner of love the Father hath bestowed upon us, that we should be called the sons of God (1 John 3:1).

But to us there is but one God, the Father, of whom are all things, and we in him (1 Cor. 8:6).

And truly our fellowship is with the Father, and with his Son Jesus Christ (1 John 1:3).

Thou shalt guide me with thy counsel, and afterward receive me to glory (Ps. 73:24).

Impressionistic Painting

Father God, my earthly canvas
Cannot capture in minute detail
   the magnitude of thy wisdom,
   the providence of thy care,
   the impartiality of thy love,
   the scope of thy justice,
   and the depth of thy mercy
     toward each penitent child.

My human understanding of thee
   as heavenly Father,
Though only an impressionistic painting
   of thy marvelous reality,
Adds meaning and security to life.

Glimpses . . .

Behold, what manner of love the Father hath bestowed upon us, that we should be called the sons of God (1 John 3:1).

Every good gift and every perfect gift is from above, and cometh down from the Father of lights, with whom is no variableness, neither shadow of turning (Jas. 1:17).

Be ye therefore merciful, as your Father also is merciful (Luke 6:36).

After this manner therefore pray ye: Our Father which art in heaven, Hallowed be thy name (Matt. 6:9).

Fear not, little flock; for it is your Father's good pleasure to give you the kingdom (Luke 12:32).

Like as a father pitieth his children, so the Lord pitieth them that fear him (Ps. 103:13).

For ye shall go out with joy, and be led forth with peace (Isa. 55:12).

Full Shadow

Are you here, Father,
In this agonizing hour of grief?
I need you so!
Surely you are near
To help me handle this.

Can it be that my eyes
   are momentarily blinded by
   tears of grief and rebellion
And cannot see that you're so very near
   in this great time of need
That I stand within
   the *full shadow* of thy presence?

Glimpses . . .

He that dwelleth in the secret place of the most High shall abide under the shadow of the Almighty (Ps. 91:1).

The Lord is nigh unto them that are of a broken heart (Ps. 34:18).

Rest in the Lord, and wait patiently for him (Ps. 37:7).

God is our refuge and strength, a very present help in trouble (Ps. 46:1).

Then they cry unto the Lord in their trouble, and he bringeth them out of their distresses (Ps. 107:28).

Because thou hast been my help, therefore in the shadow of thy wings will I rejoice (Ps. 63:7).

He healeth the broken in heart, and bindeth up their wounds (Ps. 147:3).

Trust

Father, my every glimpse of Thee
   has shown that thou art
     perfect love, goodness, and truth,
That thou art unchanging,
And that thy mercies fail not.

Although thy majesty towers far above,
Thou hast bent down to visit me
   in my humble house of dust
And revealed thy infinite love and care.

Thou hast shown me that I can
   safely *trust* you, Father,
     with every experience of life,
Even though I do not really understand.

Glimpses . . .

He that trusteth in the Lord, mercy shall compass him about (Ps. 32:10).

How excellent is thy loving kindness, O God! therefore the children of men put their trust under the shadow of thy wings (Ps. 36:7).

We trust in the living God, who is the Saviour of all men, specially of those that believe (1 Tim. 4:10).

The Lord is thy shade upon thy right hand (Ps. 121:5).

Thou wilt keep him in perfect peace, whose mind is stayed on thee: because he trusteth in thee (Isa. 26:3).

And we know that all things work together for good to them that love God, to them who are the called according to his purpose (Rom. 8:28).

He shall not be afraid of evil tidings: his heart is fixed, trusting in the Lord (Ps. 112:7).

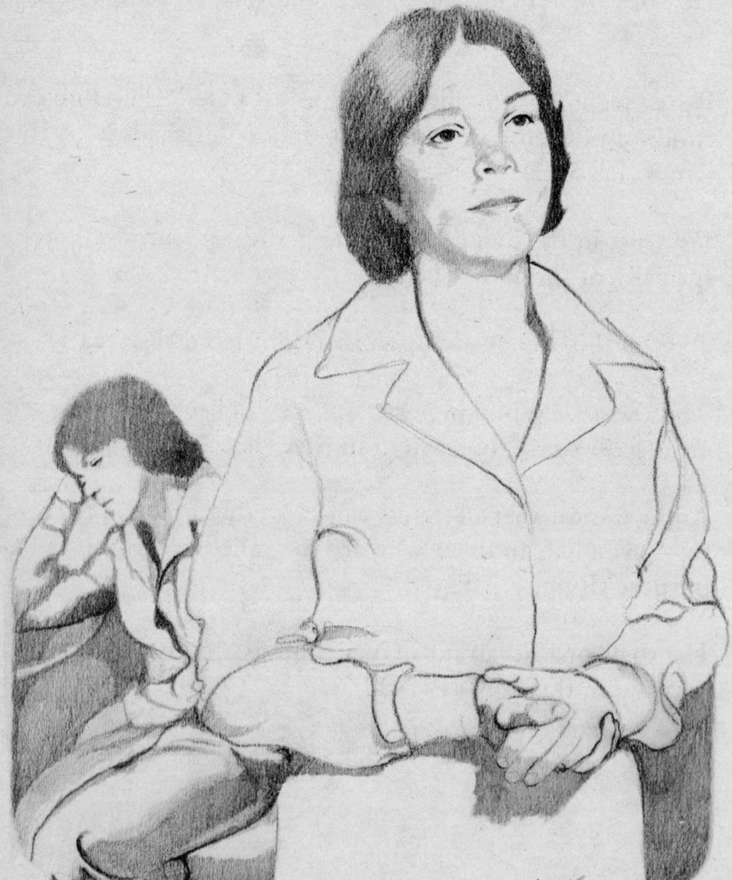
N Long

A Glimpse of Myself

So foolish was I, and ignorant (Ps. 73:22).

Desire that ye might be filled with the knowledge of his will in all wisdom and spiritual understanding; That ye might walk worthy of the Lord unto all pleasing, being fruitful in every good work, and increasing in the knowledge of God (Col. 1:9–10).

Grafted

Lord Jesus, I'm discontent
   with my sinful, scrawny self.
My body is sturdy indeed,
But my life bears no ripening fruit.

Please graft upon my trunk
A new and finer self
   that will mature and bear fruit—

Thus saving me from
   the lostness of mere sin sick existence
And saving me for
   healthy, full, abundant life.

Glimpses . . .

Abide in me, and I in you. As the branch cannot bear fruit of itself, except it abide in the vine; no more can ye, except ye abide in me (John 15:4).

Wherefore by their fruits ye shall know them (Matt. 7:20).

Herein is my Father glorified, that ye bear much fruit; so shall ye be my disciples (John 15:8).

Ye have not chosen me, but I have chosen you, and ordained you, that ye should go and bring forth fruit, and that your fruit should remain (John 15:16).

But the fruit of the Spirit is love, joy, peace, longsuffering, gentleness, goodness, faith, Meekness, temperance: against such there is no law (Gal. 5:22–23).

I am come that they might have life, and that they might have it more abundantly (John 10:10).

Ebb Tide

How smug I felt, O God,
Thinking all ugliness and sin
   are safely obscured
   by life's high tide.

Suddenly I am aware
That nothing is hidden from thee.
With one swift, inevitable pull,
Life becomes low tide
And all is revealed:
   cluttered garbage of discarded pleasure,
   treacherous coral reefs of greed and dishonesty,
   pollution of self-seeking,
   sharp shells of jealousy and envy.

Forgive me, God;
With this fresh awareness
Grant me courage to live life
In such a way that I shall not dread
   ebb tide's disclosure.

Glimpses . . .

God shall bring every work into judgment, with every secret thing, whether it be good, or whether it be evil (Eccl. 12:14).

I the Lord search the heart, I try the reins, even to give every man according to his ways, and according to the fruit of his doings (Jer. 17:10).

So then every one of us shall give account of himself to God (Rom. 14:12).

Every man shall receive his own reward according to his own labour (1 Cor. 3:8).

Every idle word that men shall speak, they shall give account thereof in the day of judgment (Matt. 12:36).

By thy words thou shalt be justified, and by thy words thou shalt be condemned (Matt. 12:37).

Scrabble

As in the game of Scrabble,
I hold some few letters
And pose the problem
　of spelling a word
　　by adding them
To what is already there.

Likewise, I hold the pieces of my life
　and confront the task
　　of giving meaning to them
As I add my own contribution to mankind.

Grant me wisdom, Lord,
　to discern the place to put my life
And courage so to live
　that my life spells out its convictions.

Glimpses . . .

The fear of the Lord is the beginning of wisdom: a good understanding have all they that do his commandments (Ps. 111:10).

A wise man will hear, and will increase learning; and a man of understanding shall attain unto wise counsel (Prov. 1:5).

See then that ye walk circumspectly, not as fools, but as wise, Redeeming the time, because the days are evil. Wherefore be ye not unwise, but understanding what the will of the Lord is (Eph. 5:15–17).

Brethren, be not children in understanding: howbeit in malice be ye children, but in understanding be men (1 Cor. 14:20).

Ye shall know the truth, and the truth shall make you free (John 8:32).

But speaking the truth in love, may grow up into him in all things, which is the head, even Christ (Eph. 4:15).

Bright Lights of Happiness

Like a moth,
   there is within me
      an instinct for pursuing
         the bright lights of happiness.

Fascinated by some gay, artificial light,
I hover there and beat my wings against it
   till I am nearly destroyed.

Seeing this weakness, Lord,
I implore thy help in discerning between
   the beckoning brightness
      of earthly thrills
And the glowing intensity of eternal values.

Glimpses . . .

So foolish was I and ignorant (Ps. 73:22).

But seek ye first the kingdom of God, and his righteousness; and all these things shall be added unto you (Matt. 6:33).

Then spake Jesus again unto them saying, I am the light of the world: he that followeth me shall not walk in darkness, but shall have the light of life (John 8:12).

But he that doeth truth cometh to the light, that his deeds may be made manifest, that they are wrought in God (John 3:21).

Then said they unto him, Lord, evermore give us this bread. And Jesus said unto them, I am the bread of life: he that cometh to me shall never hunger; and he that believeth on me shall never thirst (John 6:34–35).

I pray not that thou shouldest take them out of the world, but that thou shouldest keep them from the evil (John 17:15).

Conscience

Conscience is the built-in
   alarm clock
For life's journey.

Lord, show me how to set it
   in accordance with thy laws
So it will sound off loudly
   when I meet temptation

And automatically reset itself
   for every confrontation
     with evil.

Glimpses . . .

Having a good conscience; that whereas they speak evil of you, as of evildoers, they may be ashamed that falsely accuse your good conversation in Christ (1 Pet. 3:16).

Providing for honest things, not only in the sight of the Lord, but also in the sight of men (2 Cor. 8:21).

My righteousness I hold fast, and will not let it go: my heart shall not reproach me so long as I live (Job 27:6).

And herein do I exercise myself, to have always a conscience void of offence toward God, and toward men (Acts 24:16).

I say the truth in Christ, I lie not, my conscience also bearing me witness in the Holy Ghost (Rom. 9:1).

And Paul, earnestly beholding the council said, Men and brethren, I have lived in all good conscience before God until this day (Acts 23:1).

Christian Character

Am I just a limp rag doll, O Lord,
A plaything in the hands of life—
Tossed about by whim and chance,
Loved in rare moments of pleasure
Then suddenly dropped or ignored?

Not so? No unblinking eyes and
　silly painted smile?
No flimsy sawdust legs and mind?

I'm a viable, living being
　infused with the potential of
　　Christian character,
Which gives power to respond creatively
And determine one's own course
　through life's handling.

Glimpses . . .

That we henceforth be no more children, tossed to and fro, and carried about with every wind of doctrine, by the sleight of men, and cunning craftiness, whereby they lie in wait to deceive; But speaking the truth in love, may grow up into him in all things, which is the head, even Christ (Eph. 4:14–15).

I can do all things through Christ which strengtheneth me (Phil. 4:13).

That he would grant you, according to the riches of his glory, to be strengthened with might by his Spirit in the inner man (Eph. 3:16).

Put on the whole armour of God, that ye may be able to stand against the wiles of the devil (Eph. 6:11).

We are troubled on every side, yet not distressed; we are perplexed, but not in despair; Persecuted, but not forsaken; cast down, but not destroyed (2 Cor. 4:8–9).

Oil of Laughter

Laughter oils life's squeaking joints!

Weighted heavily with pompous pride
And overburdened with nagging, needless worry,
Life drags creakingly along.
Sometimes rust even forms
   when life is left outside
      in downpours of self-pity!

But if the oil of laughter
   is gently applied,
It helps restore healthy, working order
   once again.

(Could it be that God,
Who stocked life's shelves with laughter,
Stands nearby laughing with me?)

Glimpses . . .

Then was our mouth filled with laughter and our tongue with singing (Ps. 126:2).

A merry heart doeth good like a medicine: but a broken spirit drieth the bones (Prov. 17:22).

A merry heart maketh a cheerful countenance: but by sorrow of the heart the spirit is broken (Prov. 15:13).

A time to weep, and a time to laugh; a time to mourn, and a time to dance (Eccl. 3:4).

All the days of the afflicted are evil: but he that is of a merry heart hath a continual feast (Prov. 15:15).

Thou hast put gladness in my heart (Ps. 4:7).

Conservation

Life is eroded by conformity
   to this world alone.
Furrows of selfish pleasure are vertical,
   and the downhill rush
      of sin and self-seeking
Disintegrates one's being.

But you have provided the way, Lord,
   to check life's erosion
      and to conserve one's worth.

Careful planting of thy eternal truths
And contour plowing of right relationships
Can help stem earth's onslaught;
And the fertile soil of one's finer self,
   no longer uselessly washed away,
Is conserved to help bear fruit on earth.

Glimpses . . .

The law of his God is in his heart; none of his steps shall slide (Ps. 37:31).

I delight to do thy will, O my God: yea, thy law is within my heart (Ps. 40:8).

Behold, thou desirest truth in the inward parts: and in the hidden part thou shalt make me to know wisdom (Ps. 51:6).

Righteousness shall go before him; and shall set us in the way of his steps (Ps. 85:13).

Thy word have I hid in mine heart, that I might not sin against thee (Ps. 119:11).

Let my heart be sound in thy statutes (Ps. 119:80).

Order my steps in thy word: and let not any iniquity have dominion over me (Ps. 119:133).

Eclipse

Doubt has eclipsed
  my sight of thee, O God.
Warmth is gone; darkness engulfs.

I cannot stay like this—
  cowed and stumbling,
    trembling and dismayed.

I must force myself to rise
  and move onward,
Knowing that you are still there,
  Eternal God,
Though momentarily obscured.

This darkness of doubt will pass,
And in the growing light of renewed faith
I shall glimpse thee again!

Glimpses . . .

O my God, my soul is cast down within me (Ps. 42:6).

We wait for light, but behold obscurity; for brightness, but we walk in darkness (Isa. 59:9).

Why art thou cast down, O my soul? and why art thou disquieted within me? hope thou in God: for I shall yet praise him for the help of his countenance (Ps. 42:5).

Wherein ye greatly rejoice, though now for a season, if need be, ye are in heaviness through manifold temptations (1 Pet. 1:6).

But they that wait upon the Lord shall renew their strength (Isa. 40:31).

And he said unto them, Why are ye so fearful? how is it that ye have no faith? (Mark 4:40).

Lord, I believe; help thou mine unbelief (Mark 9:24).

Blueprint

Teach me how to read
   your blueprint for my life, O Lord,
     and build accordingly.
Busily but haphazardly,
   I've sawed and hammered every day;
But it's like adding rooms here and there
   with no central plan.

Help me grasp the design which you,
   the Architect of Life,
     foresaw.

Imprint it indelibly upon my mind
That I might follow each detail,
Knowing that only such a structure
Can stand earth's onslaught.

Glimpses . . .

Teach me to do thy will; for thou art my God (Ps. 143:10).

Therefore whosoever heareth these sayings of mine, and doeth them, I will liken him unto a wise man, which built his house upon a rock; And the rain descended, and the floods came, and the winds blew, and beat upon that house; and it fell not: for it was founded upon a rock (Matt. 7:24–25).

For we are labourers together with God: ye are God's husbandry, ye are God's building. According to the grace of God which is given unto me, as a wise masterbuilder, I have laid the foundation, and another buildeth thereon. But let every man take heed how he buildeth thereon. For other foundation can no man lay than that is laid, which is Jesus Christ (1 Cor. 3:9–11).

Know ye not that ye are the temple of God, and that the Spirit of God dwelleth in you? (1 Cor. 3:16).

Key of C

In my spiritual immaturity,
I've tried to play all of
   life's music
      in the key of C,
Keeping it easy and uncomplicated.

But life isn't like that at all;
And many of its difficult passages
   require other key signatures,
Encompassing the flats of discouragement
And the sharps of higher aspiration.

I want to grow, Lord, and learn other scales.
I'm no longer afraid
   to face the flats
      or to seek the sharps.

Teach me.

Glimpses . . .

But grow in grace, and in the knowledge of our Lord and Saviour Jesus Christ (2 Pet. 3:18).

As newborn babes, desire the sincere milk of the word, that ye may grow thereby (1 Pet. 2:2).

I can do all things through Christ which strengtheneth me (Phil. 4:13).

That we henceforth be no more children, tossed to and fro, and carried about with every wind of doctrine, by the sleight of men, and cunning craftiness, whereby they lie in wait to deceive; But speaking the truth in love, may grow up into him in all things, which is the head, even Christ (Eph. 4:14–15).

But they that wait upon the Lord shall renew their strength; they shall mount up with wings as eagles; they shall run, and not be weary; and they shall walk, and not faint (Isa. 40:31).

Apogees of Joy

My soul is at its apogee, [5] O God!
I skip with joy along a path
   ablaze with light!
   Earth's darkness is obscured;
I sense thy nearness, love, and strength
And feel a sense of peace—of harmony with thee.

I'd like to stay and worship at this height;
But life orbits on and on,
And soon its elliptical course
   will circle very close to earth again.

Yes, there will be low points in life—
   my perigees of despair—
When earth crowds in on me
   and I stumble wearily in her pollution.

Nevertheless, I shall not be overwhelmed,
For there will be the warm remembrance
   of former heights
And confident hope that
   if I but orbit in thy will,
I shall soar to apogees of joy again!

---

[5] point in orbit farthest from Earth as opposed to *perigee*, which is closest

Glimpses . . .

When I fall, I shall arise; when I sit in darkness, the Lord shall be a light unto me (Mic. 7:8).

For the kingdom of God is . . . righteousness, and peace, and joy in the Holy Ghost (Rom. 14:17).

These things have I spoken unto you, that my joy might remain in you, and that your joy might be full (John 15:11).

He giveth power to the faint; and to them that have no might he increaseth strength (Isa. 40:29).

But they that wait upon the Lord shall renew their strength; they shall mount up with wings as eagles; they shall run, and not be weary; and they shall walk, and not faint (Isa. 40:31).

The Lord God is my strength, and he will make my feet like hind's feet, and he will make me to walk upon mine high places (Hab. 3:19).

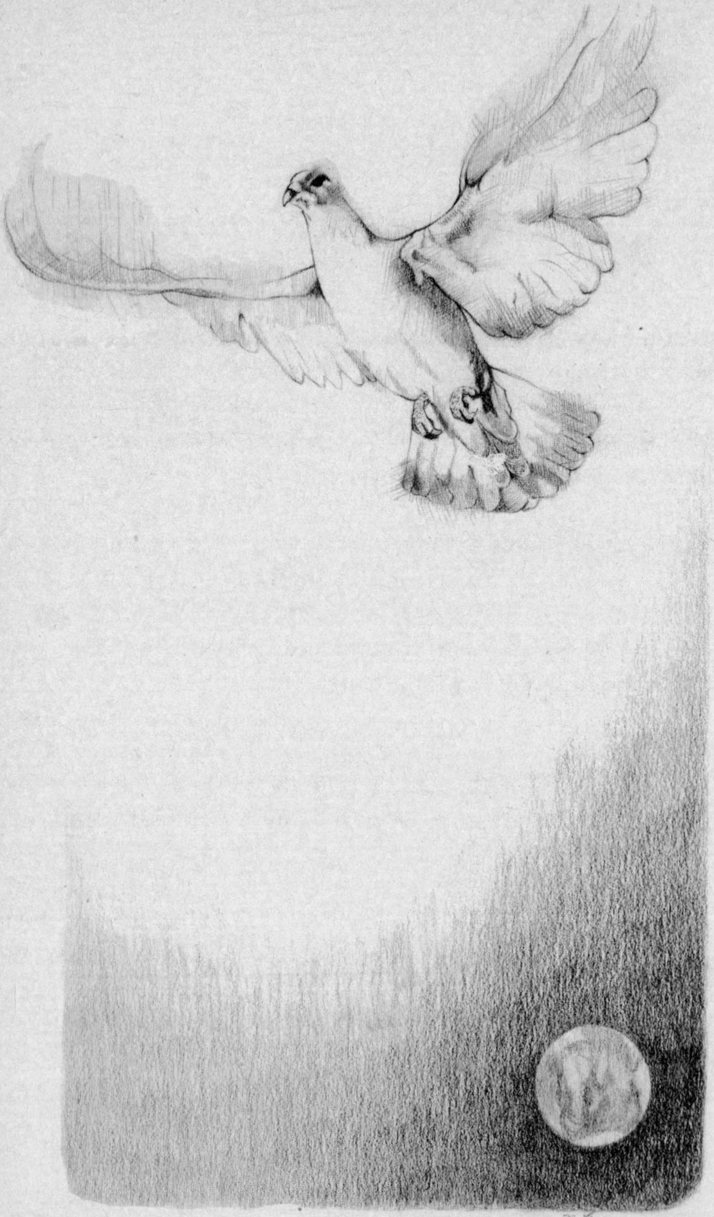

A Glimpse of Others

If a man say, I love God, and hateth his brother, he is a liar: for he that loveth not his brother whom he hath seen, how can he love God whom he hath not seen? And this commandment have we from him, That he who loveth God love his brother also (1 John 4:20–21).

Vulnerable

I know that you want me to care, Lord,
   about thy children everywhere;
But somehow the sharp edge of caring
   has been blunted by comfortable living.

It's almost as though I've immunized myself
   against the horrors of hunger and disease
      and spiritual lostness,
Knowing that if I let myself truly care
I would become vulnerable to their needs;
   and that would be costly.

Prepare me for suffering, Lord.
Help me expose my life to the
   agony of caring.
Make me spiritually vulnerable.

Glimpses . . .

But whoso hath this world's good, and seeth his brother have need, and shutteth up his bowels of compassion from him, how dwelleth the love of God in him? (1 John 3:17).

Thus speaketh the Lord of hosts, saying, Execute true judgment, and shew mercy and compassion every man to his brother (Zech. 7:9).

Bear ye one another's burdens, and so fulfil the law of Christ (Gal. 6:2).

Which now of these three, thinkest thou, was neighbour unto him that fell among the thieves? And he said, He that shewed mercy on him. Then said Jesus unto him, Go, and do thou likewise (Luke 10:36–37).

He that loveth his brother abideth in the light, and there is none occasion of stumbling in him (1 John 2:10).

Lovely Rooms

Friends, you are the keys
   with which God has unlocked
     lovely rooms within me.

They might have remained
   closed off forever
Had you not quietly turned the knob
   and stepped inside.

Through admiring your discoveries there,
You have deepened my sense
   of personal worth.

Thank you for overlooking
   the ugly, cluttered closets
     in my life
And for opening up
   my finer self.

Glimpses . . .

A friend loveth at all times (Prov. 17:17).

Can two walk together, except they be agreed? (Amos 3:3).

We took sweet counsel together and walked unto the house of God in company (Ps. 55:14).

A man that hath friends must shew himself friendly: and there is a friend that sticketh closer than a brother (Prov. 18:24).

Faithful are the wounds of a friend (Prov. 27:6).

Greater love hath no man than this, that a man lay down his life for his friends (John 15:13).

Henceforth I call you not servants; for the servant knoweth not what his lord doeth: but I have called you friends; for all things that I have heard of my Father I have made known unto you (John 15:15).

Within the Lines

Proudly he presented me his gift—
   a picture colored by kindergarten hand.
Former helter-skelter strokes
   painstakingly were placed.

"Look, Mom," he said,
"I stayed inside the lines!"

Lord, help me draw a picture
   of what is right and good.
Guide my own unsteady hand
   that I in turn might teach my child
To *live* within those lines.

Glimpses . . .

Train up a child in the way he should go: and when he is old, he will not depart from it (Prov. 22:6).

Hear, ye children, the instruction of a father, and attend to know understanding (Prov. 4:1).

My son, keep thy father's commandment, and forsake not the law of thy mother (Prov. 6:20).

Withhold not correction from the child (Prov. 23:13).

And, ye fathers, provoke not your children to wrath: but bring them up in the nurture and admonition of the Lord (Eph. 6:4).

Apply thine heart unto instruction, and thine ears to the words of knowledge (Prov. 23:12).

And thou shalt teach them diligently unto thy children, and shalt talk of them when thou sittest in thine house, and when thou walkest by the way, and when thou liest down, and when thou risest up (Deut. 6:7).

And all thy children shall be taught of the Lord; and great shall be the peace of thy children (Isa. 54:13).

Flying Buttresses

Moral principles
   are flying buttresses
Which support the structure of society.

We live together in such intricate
   individual, family, and group
      relationships

That without such strong support
   the walls would crumble.

Glimpses . . .

He hath shewed thee, O man, what is good; and what doth the Lord require of thee, but to do justly, and to love mercy, and to walk humbly with thy God? (Mic. 6:8).

These are the things that ye shall do; Speak ye every man the truth to his neighbour; execute the judgment of truth and peace in your gates (Zech. 8:16).

Providing for honest things, not only in the sight of the Lord, but also in the sight of men (2 Cor. 8:21).

The integrity of the upright shall guide them (Prov. 11:3).

Thou shalt not kill.
Thou shalt not commit adultery.
Thou shalt not steal.
Thou shalt not bear false witness against thy
    neighbour.
Thou shalt not covet (Ex. 20:13–17).

Weapons

I dare, O God, as thy Christian soldier
   to venture bravely
Against the enemies of hate
   and spiritual ignorance in this world.

Which weapons shall I use
   to win victory for thee?

Shall I drop explosive bombs of anger?
Shall I hurl grenades of condemnation?
Shall I gun down all opposition to thee?

What! You would arm me, like David,
   with a simple sling,
     to face great odds?

That sling is *love*—
The only unfailing weapon to slay
   the threatening giants
   of hostility and spiritual ignorance?

Glimpses . . .

But I say unto you, Love your enemies, bless them that curse you, do good to them that hate you, and pray for them which despitefully use you, and persecute you (Matt. 5:44).

And we have known and believed the love that God hath to us. God is love; and he that dwelleth in love dwelleth in God, and God in him (1 John 4:16).

This is my commandment, that ye love one another, as I have loved you (John 15:12).

Walk in love, as Christ also hath loved us, and hath given himself for us (Eph. 5:2).

As touching brotherly love ye need not that I write unto you: for ye yourselves are taught of God to love one another (1 Thess. 4:9).

Let brotherly love continue (Heb. 13:1).

Hygrometer

Love is somewhat like humidity.

If I fail to reach out to someone
   with loving compassion,
His life can become dry and brittle.

At times, though, I fear I've blanketed
   someone very dear
   with soggy, oppressive love
In which he cannot live and breathe with ease.

Please teach me how to read
   your hygrometer, Lord,
   in love's relationships,
That I might help others live and grow
Within the comfort index—
   ample love for security
   yet breathing room to be themselves
      and to mature.

Glimpses . . .

Let brotherly love continue (Heb. 13:1).

Walk in love, as Christ also hath loved us, and hath given himself for us an offering and a sacrifice to God for a sweetsmelling savour (Eph. 5:2).

This is my commandment, That ye love one another, as I have loved you (John 15:12).

Let love be without dissimulation (Rom. 12:9).

My little children, let us not love in word, neither in tongue; but in deed and in truth (1 John 3:18).

That their hearts might be comforted, being knit together in love (Col. 2:2).

But speaking the truth in love, may grow up into him in all things (Eph. 4:15).

Environment

Lord, I shudder to see earth's masses
   caged in the hopeless environment
     of poverty and sin.

Struggling to escape, many senselessly
   beat their wings against the
     encircling wire;
And some, who have ceased to struggle,
Fold their wings and die.

Is there no hope?
Yes! They must be shown the Way—
Christ is the Door!
Each has freedom to choose
   whether to remain only a caged prisoner
     of human circumstance
   or to unfasten the latch of faith
     and fly out
Into spiritual freedom in Christ.

Glimpses . . .

I am the door: by me if any man enter in, he shall be saved, and shall go in and out, and find pasture. The thief cometh not, but for to steal, and to kill, and to destroy: I am come that they might have life, and that they might have it more abundantly (John 10:9–10).

And Jesus said unto them, I am the bread of life: he that cometh to me shall never hunger; and he that believeth on me shall never thirst (John 6:35).

And this is the will of him that sent me, that every one which seeth the Son, and believeth on him, may have everlasting life (John 6:40).

Hearken, my beloved brethren, Hath not God chosen the poor of this world rich in faith, and heirs of the kingdom which he hath promised to them that love him? (James 2:5).

For we are labourers together with God (1 Cor. 3:9).

And ye shall know the truth, and the truth shall make you free (John 8:32).

Freedom

Surely, Lord, you placed this love of freedom
   within the embryo of life.
I find myself among the privileged free—
   yet Christ was not.

His coins bore Caesar's image.
His life and death were bound by Roman law
And yet he lived as one who's free.

His body felt earth's pull of gravity.
His feet were shackled to its dust
And yet his soul was free!

Soaring far beyond earth's finite limitations,
His spirit freely orbited in thee.
His path—thy will.

Freedom, Lord?
Christ showed us what it really is—
   Self-disciplined orderliness
     within thy will.

Glimpses . . .

And ye shall know the truth, and the truth shall make you free (John 8:32).

Submit yourselves to every ordinance of man for the Lord's sake: whether it be to the king, as supreme; Or unto governors, as unto them that are sent by him for the punishment of evildoers, and for the praise of them that do well. For so is the will of God, that with well doing ye may put to silence the ignorance of foolish men: As free, and not using your liberty for a cloak of maliciousness, but as the servants of God (1 Pet. 2:13–16).

Then saith he unto them, Render therefore unto Caesar the things which are Caesar's; and unto God the things that are God's (Matt. 22:21).

If the Son therefore shall make you free, ye shall be free indeed (John 8:36).

For the law of the Spirit of life in Christ Jesus hath made me free from the law of sin and death (Rom. 8:2).

Growing in Thy Will

Thy will, O Lord?
That not one of us should perish—
   stunted by sin
      wilted by despair
         dwarfed by hate or
            crushed by cruel inhumanity.

Thy will, O Lord?
That each should grow
   in the fertile soil
      of thy redeeming love through Christ!

Strong, sturdy lives
   deeply rooted in him
      shoot upward and outward.
Thus we grow more in thy image, Lord—
   creative and purposeful,
      loving, compassionate,
         fruit bearing.

Glimpses . . .

Even so it is not the will of your Father which is in heaven, that one of these little ones should perish (Matt. 18:14).

And this is the will of him that sent me, that every one which seeth the Son, and believeth on him, may have everlasting life: and I will raise him up at the last day (John 6:40).

Wherefore be ye not unwise, but understanding what the will of the Lord is (Eph. 5:17).

As newborn babes, desire the sincere milk of the word, that ye may grow thereby (1 Peter 2:2).

May grow up into him in all things, which is the head, even Christ (Eph. 4:15).

But grow in grace, and in the knowledge of our Lord and Saviour Jesus Christ (2 Peter 3:18).

Fulcrum

Speaking of his discovery, the lever,
Archimedes once said, "Give me a lever
   large enough and I can
     move the earth."

Can it be, Lord, that intercessory prayer
   is the lever which enables us to
     help lift the load of those far from us?
And that prayer's kneeling ground
   is the Christian's "place to stand"?

I place my prayers for the spiritual needs of
   my world upon the fulcrum of faith—
     that crucial pivot
       which empowers my effort
To affect the resistance at the other end.

What an exciting discovery, Lord,
To know that I can help personally
   through prayer
     to bring thy kingdom here on earth!
Teach me to pray, Lord!

Glimpses . . .

And all things, whatsoever ye shall ask in prayer, believing, ye shall receive (Matt. 21:22).

In whom we have boldness and access with confidence by the faith of him (Eph. 3:12).

If ye had faith as a grain of mustard seed, ye might say unto this sycamine tree, Be thou plucked up by the root and be thou planted in the sea; and it should obey you (Luke 17:6).

If ye have faith as a grain of mustard seed, ye shall say unto this mountain, Remove hence to yonder place; and it shall remove; and nothing shall be impossible unto you (Matt. 17:20).

But let him ask in faith, nothing wavering. For he that wavereth is like a wave of the sea driven with the wind and tossed (Jas. 1:6).

The effectual fervent prayer of a righteous man availeth much (Jas. 5:16).

In Jesus' Name

My prayer is ready, God, for thee,
   penned in sincerity and truth
     as I understand it
   at this point of pilgrimage.

I've stamped it with
   the price of faith.
Seal it, Holy Spirit;
   Let it hasten on its way.

But why is it still earthbound
   in my hands
And not on its heavenward
   journey to thee?

Can it be that Christ
   is the authentic postmark
   which assures delivery?

I post my prayer with thee, Lord Jesus,
   praying in thy name,
Believing thou art the Way.

Glimpses . . .

That whatsoever ye shall ask of the Father in my name, he may give it you (John 15:16).

And whatsoever ye shall ask in my name, that will I do, that the Father may be glorified in the Son (John 14:13).

If ye shall ask anything in my name, I will do it (John 14:14).

Verily, verily, I say unto you, Whatsoever ye shall ask the Father in my name, he will give it you (John 16:23).

Hitherto have ye asked nothing in my name: ask, and ye shall receive, that your joy may be full (John 16:24).

At that day ye shall ask in my name: and I say not unto you, that I will pray the Father for you: For the Father himself loveth you, because ye have loved me, and have believed that I came out from God (John 16:26–27).

Propelled

My little craft skims about, Lord,
   on the waterways of life
Sailing gaily wherever the prevailing
   winds of whim may blow.
Too often, I fear, they rush me in and out
   of the same ports—
Home, church, school, and friends.

Sometimes, though, I glimpse the haunting look
   of loneliness and futility
      upon faces of those I pass
But quickly sail beyond their view.

You saw the multitudes, Lord Jesus,
   and were moved with compassion
      toward them.

Stir up within me the breeze of compassion
   which can propel my little craft
      into those ports where there is
         deep need for love and help.

Glimpses . . .

But when he saw the multitudes, he was moved with compassion on them, because they fainted, and were scattered abroad, as sheep having no shepherd (Matt. 9:36).

Finally, be ye all of one mind, having compassion one of another, love as brethren, be pitiful, be courteous (1 Peter 3:8).

Thus speaketh the Lord of hosts, saying, Execute true judgment, and shew mercy and compassions every man to his brother (Zech. 7:9).

Bear ye one another's burdens, and so fulfil the law of Christ (Gal. 6:2).

But whoso hath this world's good, and seeth his brother have need, and shutteth up his bowels of compassion from him, how dwelleth the love of God in him? (1 John 3:17).

Shoes of Discipleship

I want to be thy disciple, Lord,
   and walk with thee.
I'm ready with shoes
   for every occasion of our journey:

Dainty heels for walking down
   cathedral aisles,
Rain boots for stormy weather,
Sturdy shoes for stony paths,
Sandals for happy, joyous ways.

These will not do, you say?
I'm cumbered with too many?
What must I carry then?

The single pair of shoes
   for Christian discipleship
     is *love*?

Then fit them to my feet, Lord Jesus,
   and teach me how to walk
     in love everywhere.

Spiritual Hearing Aid

Earth's noise drowns out
   the still, small voice of God,
Who does not shout above its din;
And I am deaf to heaven's tones.

Be my spiritual hearing aid,
   Holy Spirit,
And tune my ears
   to hear God speak
      along life's way.

Glimpses . . .

And they were all filled with the Holy Ghost, and they spake the word of God with boldness (Acts 4:31).

Now the God of hope fill you with all joy and peace in believing, that ye may abound in hope, through the power of the Holy Ghost (Rom. 15:13).

But ye shall receive power, after that the Holy Ghost is come upon you (Acts 1:8).

And hereby we know that he abideth in us, by the Spirit which he hath given us (1 John 3:24).

But the Comforter, which is the Holy Ghost, whom the Father will send in my name, he shall teach you all things, and bring all things to your remembrance, whatsoever I have said unto you (John 14:26).

Likewise the Spirit also helpeth our infirmities (Rom. 8:26).

Kinetic Energy

It's impossible, Lord,
   to live Christ's way,
      propelled by human strength alone!
It's like struggling with a single oar
   against life's overwhelming current.
Must I flounder so?

The power of steam
   and jet
      and atom
Lay dormant at man's fingertip,
   awaiting personal discovery.
Likewise, there must be vast potential energy
   available for life's pilgrimage.

Can it be that my personal discovery
   of the right relationship
      with thee, O Holy Spirit,
Empowers me to live Christ's way?

A Glimpse of the Holy Spirit

And hereby we know that he abideth in us, by the Spirit which he hath given us (1 John 3:24).

Glimpses . . .

Walk in love, as Christ also hath loved us (Eph. 5:2).

If I then, your Lord and Master, have washed your feet: ye also ought to wash one another's feet (John 13:14).

By love serve one another (Gal. 5:13).

Beloved, let us love one another: for love is of God: and every one that loveth is born of God, and knoweth God (1 John 4:7).

And this commandment have we from him, That he who loveth God love his brother also (1 John 4:21).

Ye have heard that it hath been said, Thou shalt love thy neighbour, and hate thine enemy. But I say unto you, Love your enemies (Matt. 5:43–44).

Jesus said unto him, Thou shalt love the Lord thy God with all thy heart, and with all thy soul, and with all thy mind. This is the first and great commandment. And the second is like unto it, Thou shalt love thy neighbour as thyself (Matt. 22:37–39).

Glimpses . . .

But the Comforter, which is the Holy Ghost, whom the Father will send in my name, he shall teach you all things, and bring all things to your remembrance, whatsoever I have said unto you (John 14:26).

And I will pray the Father, and he shall give you another Comforter, that he may abide with you forever (John 14:16).

For the Holy Ghost shall teach you in the same hour what ye ought to say (Luke 12:12).

The love of God is shed abroad in our hearts by the Holy Ghost which is given unto us (Rom. 5:5).

And it is the Spirit that beareth witness, because the Spirit is truth (1 John 5:6).

Tightrope of Temptation

I'm walking the tightrope
   of temptation again, Lord!
     I'm scared!

You didn't say we'd never face
   temptation,
But you promised to be with us
   and keep us from falling.

I claim that promise, Lord,
   as I fix my eyes straight
     ahead on thee
Instead of looking down.

Help me relax a bit and trust in thee,
Believing that thy Holy Spirit
   is my ready help and
     like a balancing pole in my hand
Enables me, step by step,
   to walk victoriously
     through this temptation.

Glimpses . . .

This I say then, Walk in the Spirit, and ye shall not fulfil the lust of the flesh (Gal. 5:16).

Likewise the Spirit also helpeth our infirmities (Rom. 8:26).

Wherefore let him that thinketh he standeth take heed lest he fall. There hath no temptation taken you but such as is common to man: but God is faithful, who will not suffer you to be tempted above that ye are able; but will with the temptation also make a way to escape, that ye may be able to bear it (1 Cor. 10:12–13).

The Lord knoweth how to deliver the godly out of temptations (2 Peter 2:9).

Blessed is the man that endureth temptation (Jas. 1:12).

Interpreter

I speak only earth's language, Lord.
It marks the meager boundaries
  of my mind.
How can I possibly communicate
  with the Almighty?

Can it be that you, Holy Spirit,
Are the personal interpreter
  between earth and heaven?
That you translate the deep yearnings
  of my soul poured out in prayer
Into heaven's language
  before the throne of God?

And in turn express in simple words
My listening ears can understand
God's own message for my soul?

Glimpses . . .

Likewise the Spirit also helpeth our infirmities: for we know not what we should pray for as we ought: but the Spirit itself maketh intercession for us with groanings which cannot be uttered. And he that searcheth the hearts knoweth what is the mind of the Spirit, because he maketh intercession for the saints according to the will of God (Rom. 8:26–27).

But ye, beloved, building up yourselves on your most holy faith, praying in the Holy Ghost, Keep yourselves in the love of God, looking for the mercy of our Lord Jesus Christ unto eternal life (Jude 20–21).

If ye then, being evil, know how to give good gifts unto your children: how much more shall your heavenly Father give the Holy Spirit to them that ask him? (Luke 11:13).

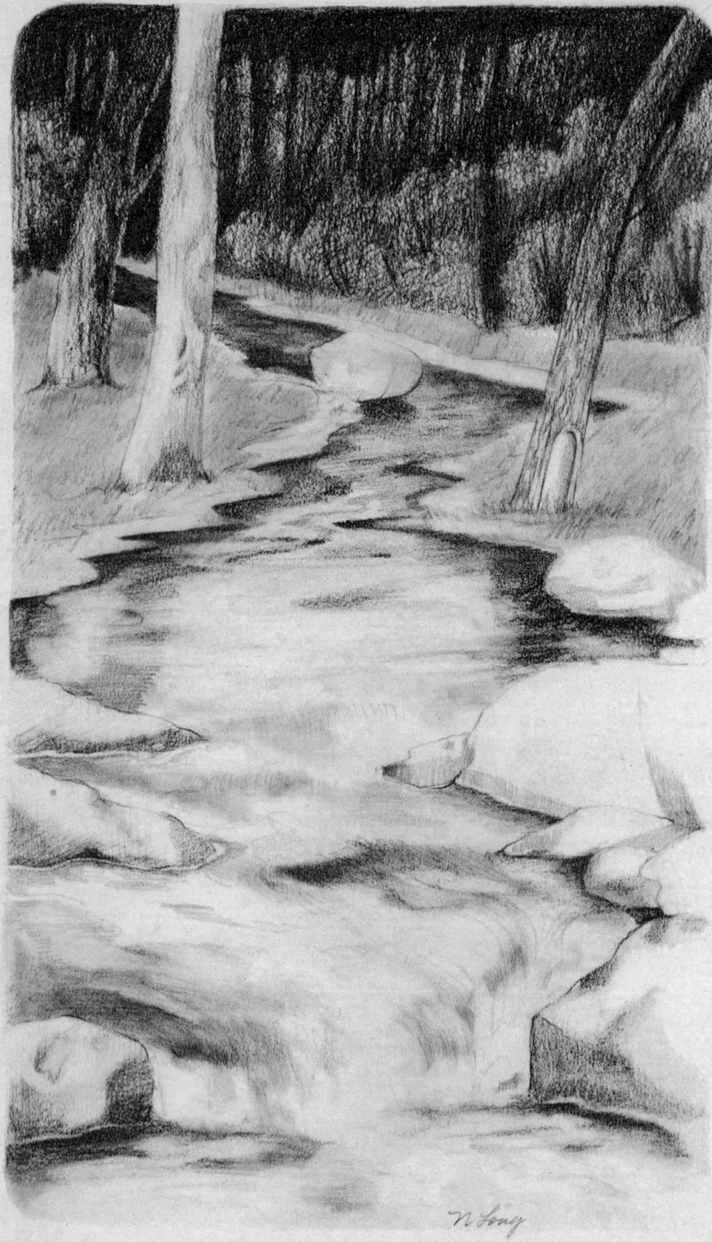

A Glimpse of the Church

Upon this rock I will build my church; and the gates of hell shall not prevail against it (Matt. 16:18).

Orchard

Lord, as a Christian,
   am I just a single tree
      struggling alone in my little plot?

You foresaw *orchards* of fruit-bearing Christians
   growing together,
      nourished and disciplined
         by thy loving care,
To more effectively feed
   this spiritually starving world?

Thy church, O Lord,
Is that orchard of fruit-bearing Christians?
Then I shall plant my life there too.

Glimpses . . .

Not forsaking the assembling of ourselves together, as the manner of some is; but exhorting one another; and so much the more, as ye see the day approaching (Heb. 10:25).

Take heed therefore unto yourselves, and to all the flock, over the which the Holy Ghost hath made you overseers, to feed the church of God, which he hath purchased with his own blood (Acts 20:28).

Ye have not chosen me, but I have chosen you, and ordained you, that ye should go and bring forth fruit, and that your fruit should remain: that whatsoever ye shall ask of the Father in my name, he may give it you (John 15:16).

That ye might walk worthy of the Lord unto all pleasing, being fruitful in every good work, and increasing in the knowledge of God (Col. 1:10).

That we should bring forth fruit unto God (Rom. 7:4).

Abide in me, and I in you. As the branch cannot bear fruit of itself, except it abide in the vine; no more can ye, except ye abide in me (John 15:4).

Money Changers

You were irate with those money changers, Lord,
   and rightly so!
Thieves they were in God's house of prayer!

But you look hurt and angry with the church today,
   Lord Jesus. Why?
Are there "money changers" still?

Can it be that I am blind to the fact
   that I and others too
Piously exchange our money
   for the blessings of a great
     church plant and program
And fail to pay the greater cost
   of love and prayer
     for all mankind—
Thus robbing them of their right
   to know thee too?

Glimpses . . .

And Jesus went into the temple of God, and cast out all them that sold and bought in the temple, and overthrew the tables of the moneychangers, and the seats of them that sold doves, And said unto them, It is written, My house shall be called the house of prayer; but ye have made it a den of thieves (Matt. 21:12–13).

Holiness becometh thine house, O Lord, for ever (Ps. 93:5).

Other sheep I have, which are not of this fold: them also I must bring, and they shall hear my voice; and they shall be one fold and one shepherd (John 10:16).

And this gospel of the kingdom shall be preached in all the world for a witness unto all nations (Matt. 24:14).

Go ye therefore, and teach all nations, baptizing them in the name of the Father, and of the Son, and of the Holy Ghost: Teaching them to observe all things whatsoever I have commanded you: and, lo, I am with you alway, even unto the end of the world. Amen (Matt. 28:19–20).

Citizens of the Kingdom

I confess, Lord, that oftentimes
   in thy kingdom here on earth
My conduct has been more like
   that of tourist
      than of citizen.

Casually, I have drifted about
   seeing its sights
      and tasting its delicacies
Without truly identifying myself
   as one of its people,
      loyal and devoted to thee.

Help me grow toward responsible
   citizenship in thy kingdom, Lord,
Shouldering my share of the work
   of doing thy will on earth.

Glimpses . . .

Ye are no more strangers and foreigners, but fellow-citizens with the saints, and of the household of God; And are built upon the foundation of the apostles and prophets, Jesus Christ himself being the chief corner stone; in whom all the building fitly framed together groweth unto an holy temple in the Lord: In whom ye also are builded together for an habitation of God through the Spirit (Eph. 2:19–22).

Ye also helping together by prayer for us (2 Cor. 1:11).

We therefore ought to receive such, that we might be fellow-helpers to the truth (3 John 8).

Now concerning the collection for the saints, as I have given order to the churches of Galatia, even so do ye. Upon the first day of the week let every one of you lay by him in store, as God hath prospered him (1 Cor. 16:1–2).

Reflecting

Earth would be dark indeed
  if there were no heavenly bodies
    to reflect light to us.

Is this thy plan, O Lord?
That all of us as Christians
Reflect the light of Christ
  to this dark world?

My own path seems very small,
But I shall endeavor to reflect thy love
  to those within it
And with my gifts and prayers
Help launch others into wider paths
Until thy light is reflected clearly
  throughout the world.

Glimpses . . .

Ye are the light of the world. A city that is set on a hill cannot be hid. Let your light so shine before men that they may see your good works, and glorify your Father which is in heaven (Matt. 5:14,16).

But ye shall receive power, after that the Holy Ghost is come upon you: and ye shall be witnesses unto me both in Jerusalem, and in all Judaea, and in Samaria, and unto the uttermost part of the earth (Acts 1:8).

For God, who commanded the light to shine out of darkness, hath shined in our hearts, to give the light of the knowledge of the glory of God in the face of Jesus Christ (2 Cor. 4:6).

For ye were sometimes darkness, but now are ye light in the Lord: walk as children of light (Eph. 5:8).

Having therefore obtained help of God, I continue unto this day, witnessing both to small and great (Acts 26:22).

Tributaries

Father God, the deep waters
  of thy love
Have flowed through our desert wastelands
  of existence
And made life bloom
  with joy and peace.

May we in turn, as Christians,
  become tributaries of thy love
That we might help channel the water of life
Into parched and thirsty lives
  throughout the earth.

Glimpses . . .

And all things are of God, who hath reconciled us to himself by Jesus Christ, and hath given to us the ministry of reconciliation. Now then we are ambassadors for Christ (2 Cor. 5:18,20).

But in all things approving ourselves as the ministers of God (2 Cor. 6:4).

Or our brethren be enquired of, they are the messengers of the churches, and the glory of Christ. Wherefore shew ye to them, and before the churches, the proof of your love (2 Cor. 8:23–24).

Now thanks be unto God, which always causeth us to triumph in Christ, and maketh manifest the savour of his knowledge by us in every place (2 Cor. 2:14).

How then shall they call on him in whom they have not believed? and how shall they believe in him of whom they have not heard? and how shall they hear without a preacher? (Rom. 10:14).

Forasmuch as ye are manifestly declared to be the epistle of Christ ministered by us, written not with ink, but with the Spirit of the living God; not in tables of stone, but in fleshy tables of the heart (2 Cor. 3:3).

Revelation

I am Alpha and Omega, the beginning and the ending, saith the Lord, which is, and which was, and which is to come, the Almighty (Rev. 1:8).

Spectrum

Almighty God,
Thou hast chosen to reveal thyself
   through earth's prism as a spectrum:
      Father, Son, and Holy Spirit.
Yet thou art still that single beam
   of pure white light
      streaming through eternity;
For thou art ONE—O GOD!

I would worship thee, Almighty God:
   Creator, Redeemer, Sustainer, Judge.
I stand in awe of the totality of thy being,
But I kneel in loving response to thee
   as Father, Son, and Holy Spirit—
Comprehending through those relationships
Something of thy love for me personally.

Thou art near,
For my soul responds to thy presence.

Glimpses . . .

O come, let us worship and bow down: let us kneel before the Lord our maker (Ps. 95:6).

The grace of the Lord Jesus Christ, and the love of God, and the communion of the Holy Ghost, be with you all (2 Cor. 13:14).

But ye, beloved, building up yourselves on your most holy faith, praying in the Holy Ghost, Keep yourselves in the love of God, looking for the mercy of our Lord Jesus Christ unto eternal life (Jude 20–21).

Go ye therefore, and teach all nations, baptizing them in the name of the Father, and of the Son, and of the Holy Ghost (Matt. 28:19).

But to us there is but one God, the Father, of whom are all things, and we in him: and one Lord Jesus Christ, by whom are all things, and we by him (1 Cor. 8:6).

I am Alpha and Omega, the beginning and the ending, saith the Lord, which is, and which was, and which is to come, the Almighty (Rev. 1:8).

Thy Shadow

Now I see more clearly, Lord!

Thy shadow here on earth
   is thy sustaining love and care,
     HEAVENLY FATHER!

And CHRIST, our Light,
leads us to Thee!

And thy SPIRIT, God,
Is our Enabler for the Way.

Help me abide in thy shadow, God,
Throughout life's small fraction
   of eternity.

Glimpses . . .

For there are three that bear record in heaven, the Father, the Word, and the Holy Ghost: and these three are one (1 John 5:7).

He that hath the Son hath life; and he that hath not the Son of God hath not life (1 John 5:12).

For God so loved the world, that he gave his only begotten Son, that whosoever believeth in him should not perish, but have everlasting life. For God sent not his Son into the world to condemn the world; but that the world through him might be saved (John 3:16–17).

Jesus saith unto him, I am the way, the truth, and the life: no man cometh unto the Father, but by me (John 14:6).

But the Comforter, which is the Holy Ghost, whom the Father will send in my name, he shall teach you all things, and bring all things to your remembrance, whatsoever I have said unto you (John 14:26).

The Spirit itself beareth witness with our spirit, that we are the children of God: And if children, then heirs; heirs of God, and joint-heirs with Christ (Rom. 8:16–17).

I will walk among you, and will be your God, and ye shall be my people (Lev. 26:12).

When Life Is Felled

When life is felled
  in earth's forest,
May its rings reveal
  continuing growth.

And when death's final process
  transforms life's earthly trunk
    into heavenly scroll,
May Christ my Redeemer
  see fit to write thereon:
Thou hast been faithful in the shadows.
Welcome to the Light!

Glimpses . . .

Behold, I shew you a mystery; We shall not all sleep, but we shall all be changed, For this corruptible must put on incorruption, and this mortal must put on immortality. O death, where is thy sting? O grave, where is thy victory? But thanks be to God, which giveth us the victory through our Lord Jesus Christ (1 Cor. 15:51,53,55,57).

Let us hold fast the profession of our faith without wavering (for he is faithful that promised) (Heb. 10:23).

If in this life only we have hope in Christ, we are of all men most miserable (1 Cor. 15:19).

Be thou faithful unto death, and I will give thee a crown of life (Rev. 2:10).

His lord said unto him, Well done, good and faithful servant . . . enter thou into the joy of thy lord (Matt. 25:23).

Epilogue

Abide under the shadow of the Almighty (Ps. 91:1).

Who is the blessed and only Potentate, the King of kings, and Lord of lords; Who only hath immortality, dwelling in the light which no man can approach unto; whom no man hath seen, nor can see: to whom be honour and power everlasting. Amen (1 Tim. 6:15–16).

And such trust have we through Christ to God-ward (2 Cor. 3:4).